Friendship cannot live w~~...~~

no ~~...~~

A Father's ~~...~~, a Brother's a comfort; a Friend is both.

A Brother may not be a Friend, but a Fri~~end~~ ~~...~~ Brother.

A true ~~...~~ Possession.

The same ~~...~~ end and Flatterer.

Promises ~~...~~ non-performance ~~...~~ emies.

Fart Wo~~...~~ : a spoonful of honey ~~...~~ than a Gallon

An ope~~...~~ ~~c~~urse; but a pr~~...~~ worse.

No bette~~...~~ prudent and

There a~~...~~ nds — an old wife, a ~~...~~ money.

If any man ~~...~~ flatter him again, tho' he were my best Friend.

If you would keep your secret from an enemy, tell it not to a friend.

'Tis better to leave for an enemy at one's death, than beg of a friend in one's life.

Be slow in chusing a friend, slower in changing.

PENN'D FOR POOR RICHARD'S ALMANACK

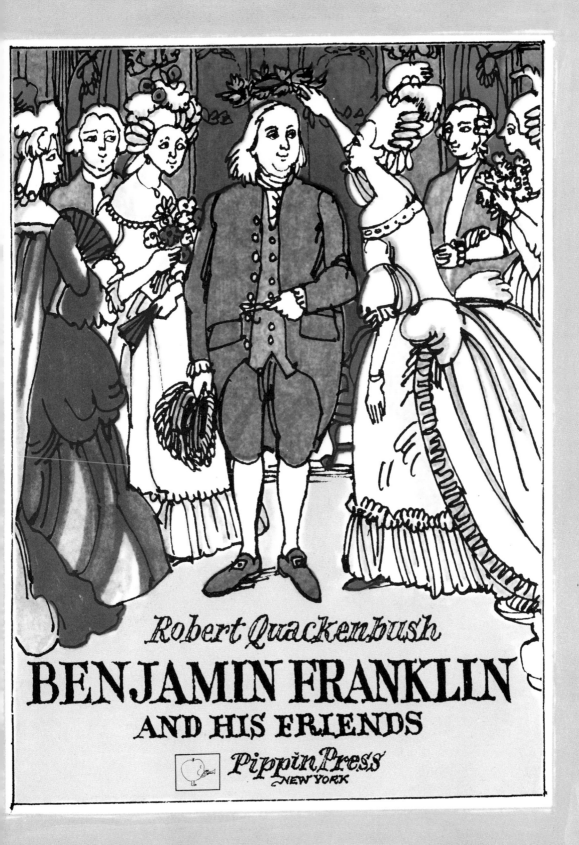

Robert Quackenbush

BENJAMIN FRANKLIN
AND HIS FRIENDS

Pippin Press
NEW YORK

Published by Pippin Press, 229 East 85th Street,
Gracie Station Box #92,
New York, N.Y. 10028

Printed in the United States by Horowitz/Rae
Book Manufacturers, Inc.
10 9 8 7 6 5 4 3 2 1

Library of Congress Cataloging-in-Publication Data

Quackenbush, Robert M.
  Benjamin Franklin and his friends / by Robert Quackenbush.
    p. cm.
  Summary: Describes the life of Benajmin Franklin, inventor,
statesman, printer, scientist, and reformer, through the friendships
he made with people of all types.
  ISBN 0-945912-14-5
    1. Franklin, Benjamin, 1706–1790—Juvenile literature.
  2. Statesmen—United States—Biography—Juvenile literature.
  3. Printers—United States—Biography—Juvenile literature.
  4. Scientists—United States—Biography—Juvenile literature.
  [1. Franklin, Benjamin, 1706–1790. 2. Statesmen. 3. Printers.
  4. Scientists.] I. Title.
  E302.6.F8033 1991
  973.3'092—dc20
    [B]   91-3960
                                                      CIP
                                                       AC

For the students
in my after-school
workshops;
with special thanks to:
Rollo Begley
Ben Bronfman
Angus Dwyer
Pearsall Helms
Tyler Hinckley
Alex Rich
Christian Werwaiss
Jordan Webb
R.Q.

1: BENJAMIN FRANKLIN AND JOHN COLLINS

There was once a boy named Benjamin Franklin. He was born in Boston, Massachusetts on January 17, 1706. Massachusetts in those days was one of thirteen colonies that were owned by the British. In Ben's house on Milk Street, there were seventeen children in the Franklin family. Ben was the fifteenth child and the last of ten sons. He was an active boy of average height, with shoulder-length brown hair and a touch of whimsy in his face. He liked to tell jokes. He loved to read and collect books. He was an excellent swimmer. He was a leader among his friends. One of his best friends was named John Collins. Ben and John liked to have debates. One time they debated about whether girls should go to school or not. Ben was for it, John was not. They wrote down their arguments. Ben's father, who had been educated in England as a child, saw what Ben had written. He praised his son for his spelling but said that he needed to improve his composition. Ben practiced and practiced to become a good writer. Little did he know at the time—nor did his father or John Collins—that one day his writings would make him famous.

WHAT HAPPENED TO JOHN COLLINS?

FRANKLIN SAID THAT ALTHOUGH JOHN COLLINS WAS A BETTER ACHIEVER AT MANY THINGS THAN HE WAS — ESPECIALLY AT MATH — HE NEVER DID WELL WHEN HE GREW UP BECAUSE HE STOPPED STUDYING AND WORKING HARD.

DID YOU KNOW THAT FRANKLIN INVENTED THE FIRST SWIM FINS?

SURE. WHEN HE WAS A BOY HE TIED WOODEN PADDLES TO HIS FEET SO HE COULD SWIM FASTER.

2: BENJAMIN FRANKLIN AND SIR WILLIAM KEITH

Ben's father Josiah and his mother Abiah wanted him to have an education. But they could afford to pay for only two years of school. At the end of the two years, Ben went to work in his father's candle and soap making shop. Then, when he was twelve, he became an apprentice to his brother James, a printer. He learned about printing books and newspapers. By the time he was seventeen he wanted to be on his own. He left his apprenticeship and Boston, and went to Philadelphia to find work. He was hired by a printer named Samuel Kleimer. While at Kleimer's shop, Ben became acquainted with the governor of Pennsylvania, Sir William Keith. Keith encouraged Ben to open his own printing shop. He wanted Ben to go to England to buy equipment. He said that a letter would be waiting for him in London that would provide him with money to buy what he needed. But when Ben arrived, the letter was not there. He found out that Keith was a dreamer who made promises that he could not keep. Even so, Ben decided to stay in London. He saw that marvelous opportunities awaited him there. Printing methods, for example, were far more advanced than they were in America. He might never have gotten to London if he had not known Keith.

Franklin immediately found work in Samuel Palmer's, one of London's finest printing houses. He soon became a master printer. In his spare time he visited libraries, went to the theatre, and swam in the River Thames. His swimming ability so impressed Londoners that he was asked to open a swimming school. But he never got around to doing that. He left England after two years. Back in Philadelphia he worked for a while with Samuel Kleimer, his former employer, at greatly increased wages. Then, in 1728, at the age of twenty-two, he opened his own printing shop. He worked day and night, usually seven days a week. His industriousness paid off. He became the official printer for Pennsylvania, which meant that he printed the money and important documents of the colony. As busy as he was, Franklin, as always, made friends easily. He organized ten of his friends—young men with alert minds like his—to meet as a discussion group on Friday evenings. This lively group became known as the Leather Apron Club because most of its members wore the work apron of artisans. The members discussed ways they could help their community. At Franklin's suggestion, they started lending books to the public for a small fee. Thus the first lending library in America began in 1730.

4: BENJAMIN FRANKLIN AND DEBORAH READ

As Franklin's printing business continued to flourish, he wished to marry. He set out to court Deborah Read. She was the daughter of the family Franklin had stayed with when he first came to Philadelphia. Their friendship blossomed into romance. They were married on September 1, 1730. Three children were born to them—two sons, named William and Francis, and a daughter named Sarah. Even with his added family responsibilities, Franklin continued to serve his community. He became postmaster of the city of Philadelphia. He established a fire company for Philadelphia and America's first free hospital. He founded a school which became the University of Pennsylvania. At the same time he expanded his business. With Deborah's help, he added a stationery and book store to his printing shop. He also printed a successful newspaper called *The Pennsylvania Gazzette*. His marriage, his happy family life, and the admiration and respect of the people of Philadelphia greatly inspired his creative activities.

Franklin's next publishing venture after his newspaper was an almanac. An almanac notes the holidays, the tides, the cycles of the moon, the best time for planting different crops, and all kinds of useful tidbits of information. Franklin developed a witty character named Poor Richard to appear throughout. He entitled the book *Poor Richard's Almanack*. It became an immediate success in the colonies and abroad. Nearly every home had one. In addition to the standard information, it was filled with "Sayings of Poor Richard" that readers loved. Franklin wrote them himself, of course. Poor Richard became the spokesman for maxims like "Fish and visitors stink in three days" and "A penny saved is a penny earned." A new edition of *Poor Richard's Almanack* was published in the colonies every year from 1733-1758. Much of the wisdom Franklin put in Poor Richard's mouth dealt with the importance of working hard and saving money. The French especially took everything *Bonhomme Richard* (the French translation of "Good man Richard") said to heart. His creator became something of a hero to them. This admiration helped America to win its freedom from the British in the Revolutionary War decades later.

6: BENJAMIN FRANKLIN AND DR. ARCHIBALD SPENCER

In 1746, Franklin became friends with Dr. Archibald Spencer, a Scottish lecturer who did electrical experiments. Franklin urged Spencer to sell him his apparatus. Two years later, at age forty-two, Franklin announced his retirement from business to devote more time to do experimenting and inventing. During his lifetime he invented many things. He invented the Franklin stove (1742), which improved heating for homes. He invented biofocals (1784), which made it possible for people to see near and far with the same pair of eye glasses. But Franklin is best remembered for his experiments with electricity. One stormy night in June 1752, with his son William at his side, he flew a kite that had a pointed metal piece on top. At the base of the kite string, he attached a metal key. A small lightning discharge struck the kite and traveled down the kite string to the key. Franklin lightly touched the key with the knuckles of one hand and saw a spark. This was proof that lightning and electricity are the same. With that, he invented the lightning rod to protect homes during electrical storms. But what a dangerous experiment! A larger flash of lightning might have electrocuted him, as it did a Russian scientist who tried Franklin's experiment that same year.

FRANKLIN AND SPENCER: WHAT A TEAM!

FRANKLIN SAID: "A FATHER'S A TREASURE; A BROTHER'S A COMFORT; A FRIEND IS BOTH."

DID YOU KNOW THAT FRANKLIN NEVER PATENTED HIS INVENTIONS? HE BELIEVED THAT THEY BELONGED TO THE PEOPLE.

HOW GENEROUS!

DR. ARCHIBALD SPENCER

Franklin wrote about his experiments with electricity to a friend, Peter Collinson, a London merchant. They had been corresponding with one another for over twenty years. Collinson saved Franklin's letters about the experiments and soon afterward had them published in England and France in a pamphlet entitled *Experiments and Observations on Electricity, made at Philadelphia in America*. Collinson's efforts firmly established Franklin's reputation throughout Europe as America's leading scientist. Franklin received many honors and awards. His fame spread throughout the colonies. He was elected by the General Assembly—the local governing body of the colony—to serve as a representative for Philadelphia. He was appointed postmaster general for all the colonies. In 1754, he was chosen as a delegate at a meeting of the six colonies in Albany, New York to discuss their common defense. At the Albany Congress, Franklin proposed a plan for a colonial union. His plan was rejected. He was decades ahead of his time. Even earlier, Franklin, a defender of the rights of man from his youth, declared:

> *Those who would give up essential liberty*
> *to purchase a little temporary safety*
> *deserve neither liberty nor safety.*

8: BENJAMIN FRANKLIN AND LORD RICHARD HOWE AND HOWE'S SISTER, LADY HOWE

Between 1757 and 1762 and between 1764 and 1775, Franklin served as representative for the American colonies in England. Deborah did not go because Franklin needed her to be in charge of the home while he was away, especially during those years when their youngest child was growing up. Franklin's mission was to attempt to settle disputes between the Americans and the British. Many of the disputes had to do with unfair taxes that the British attempted to place on the colonies. In 1775, the British placed a tax on tea that they exported to America. In protest, colonists in Massachusetts dressed as Indians and tossed shipments of tea from British cargo ships into Boston Harbor. "The Boston Tea Party" enraged the British. There were further uprisings in the colonies. In a final effort to prevent war, Franklin drafted a list of conditions for peace to the king's ministers, which included a motion for no taxation without representation. During this time, Franklin became friends with Lord Richard Howe, a rear admiral and a member of the British Parliament. Lord Howe's sister, Lady Howe, invited Franklin for evenings of chess at Lord Howe's. Soon Franklin realized that such games were a trick. Lord Howe used them in an attempt to bribe Franklin to rewrite his peace conditions in favor of the British. Franklin refused to do it.

THAT WAS A SNEAKY THING FOR HOWE TO DO.

FRANKLIN SAID: "AN OPEN FOE MAY PROVE A CURSE; BUT A PRETENDED FRIEND IS WORSE."

IT MUST HAVE BEEN VERY HARD FOR FRANKLIN TO BE AWAY FROM HIS FAMILY FOR ALL THOSE YEARS.

HE TOOK HIS SON WILLIAM WITH HIM ON THE FIRST TRIP AND HIS GRANDSONS WENT WITH HIM ON OTHER TRIPS.

9: BENJAMIN FRANKLIN AND THOMAS JEFFERSON

In the spring of 1775, Franklin sailed home because Deborah had died and war was coming. While he was still crossing the ocean, the first shots of the Revolutionary War were fired at Lexington and Concord, in Massachusetts, on April 19, 1775. In May, Franklin arrived at last in Philadelphia. He was immediately elected a member of the Second Continental Congress which met to declare the colonies a free and independent nation. Thomas Jefferson was also a member of the Congress. Franklin and Jefferson became good friends because they were both famous writers and inventors. When Jefferson was asked to draft a Declaration of Independence, he asked Franklin for suggestions. Most of the suggestions were minor, but one has proved enduring and memorable. Where Jefferson wrote, "We hold these truths to be sacred and undeniable," Franklin crossed out the last three words and added simply, "self-evident." Then on July 4, 1776 the colonies announced their declaration to the world. Within a week the British sent war ships to America. Lord Richard Howe commanded one of the fleets. He sent a friendly letter to Franklin to use his influence to prevent war and promote peace. Franklin's reply supported Jefferson's bold words in the Declaration. He urged Howe to turn back. But his reply went unheeded. The war was on.

FRANKLIN AND JEFFERSON: NOW THAT WAS A REAL FRIENDSHIP!

BUT WHAT ABOUT HOWE COMING BACK INTO FRANKLIN'S LIFE AGAIN?

FRANKLIN SAID: "BEWARE OF MEAT TWICE BOIL'D, AND AN OLD FOE RECONCIL'D."

10: BENJAMIN FRANKLIN AND THE PEOPLE OF FRANCE

In December 1776, Franklin was sent by the Continental Congress as minister to France to seek money and supplies to help support the American Revolution. When he arrived in France he was wearing a fur hat and simple clothing. At last the French got to meet their hero—the creator of Poor Richard. They were not disappointed in what they saw. He fit their romantic idea of an American—a kind, simple man who looked as if he came from the backwoods. There was scarcely a person in France who did not welcome him and consider him a friend. He talked to the rulers about how England, France's traditional enemy, would be all-powerful if the colonies were defeated. To the businessmen, he talked about the value of trading with the Americans directly, if America were free of British control. To the people he talked about liberty and freedom. Wherever he went he was greeted with warmth and enthusiasm. Soon his portrait hung over fireplaces in nearly every French home. Miniature paintings of him appeared on rings, lockets, and snuff boxes. Women created hairstyles to look like Franklin wearing his fur hat. Franklin's popularity made him confident that the French would help the Americans gain freedom from the British.

11: BENJAMIN FRANKLIN AND BARON VON STEUBEN

Among Franklin's tasks as minister to the French court, was to screen foreign officers who wanted to serve in the Continental—or American—Army during the Revolutionary War. Nearly every European who desired a commission in the army came to Franklin for a recommendation. Franklin did not feel that many of them were qualified. He wrote to George Washington, Commanding General of the Continental Army. He apologized for the fact that there were so few qualified applicants. But one applicant impressed him very much and they became friends. His name was Baron Friedrich von Steuben. Von Steuben was a German captain who received his rigorous military training in Prussia in the service of King Frederick the Great. Franklin knew that he would be a welcome addition to Washington's army. He wrote General Washington a glowing letter of recommendation. Washington was impressed by the letter and so was Congress. On the strength of Franklin's faith and trust in his new friend's ability, von Steuben was assigned by Congress to Washington's headquarters at Valley Forge. Franklin was right. Von Steuben proved to be a crack drillmaster. He succeeded in turning Washington's fledgling troops into a disciplined fighting force.

12: BENJAMIN FRANKLIN AND MARQUES DE LAFAYETTE AND JOHN PAUL JONES

Another foreign officer who distinguished himself in the Revolutionary War was France's Marquis de Lafayette. Franklin and he became friends in Paris before Lafayette sailed for America. Backers of Lafayette wanted to send the young nobleman a large sum of money to help support him overseas. But they knew he spent money freely and that he would soon go through it all. Franklin handled the matter tactfully. He wrote to Washington. He suggested that Washington dole out the money in small sums to the Marquis with "friendly advise" on how to spend it. Then in February 1779, Lafayette returned to Paris on leave and visited Franklin. Franklin, Lafayette and John Paul Jones, an American naval officer, made plans to attack England in an attempt to shorten the war. Franklin became friends with Jones by helping him to obtain a ship from the French government. Jones named the ship *Bonhomme Richard* after Franklin's Poor Richard. In the plans they made, Lafayette was to command the ground troops. Franklin gave sound suggestions about how Lafayette should employ his cavalry after he landed. The ground attack did not take place, but a sea battle went ahead according to plan. On September 23, 1779, Jones won his famous victory over the British ship of war *Serapis*.

13: BENJAMIN FRANKLIN AND KING LOUIS XVI AND QUEEN MARIE ANTOINETTE

Meanwhile, American revolutionary forces were steadily losing ground. The Continental Congress was running out of money. Unpaid soldiers were mutinying. Washington wrote Franklin saying that more money was needed or America would have to surrender to the British. Franklin appealed to the king and queen of France. Finally, in 1781, King Louis agreed to give money to the Americans. With French support, America's forces gained the morale and strength they needed. They were able to win the Revolutionary War. For most Americans, the war ended on October 19, 1781, when General Cornwallis surrendered at Yorktown. But for Franklin, it continued for two more years, while he endeavored to bargain for peace. At last, on September 3, 1783, a peace treaty was signed between England and the American and French allies. "May we never see another war!" said Franklin. "For in my opinion there was never a good war or a bad peace." Upon signing the peace treaty, Franklin requested that Congress release him from his ministry. He was in his late seventies. He wanted to spend his remaining years at home living with his daughter and grandchildren. Nine weeks later, after saying goodbye to his many friends in France, Franklin sailed home.

TWO YEARS TO BARGAIN FOR PEACE?

WHAT A LOT OF WORK.

FRANKLIN SAID:"WHEN A FRIEND DEALS WITH A FRIEND, LET THE BARGAIN BE CLEAR AND WELL PENN'D THAT THEY MAY CONTINUE FRIENDS TO THE END."

When Franklin arrived back in America, he was greeted as an extraordinary hero. He landed in Philadelphia among the booms of cannon salutes and clangs of pealing church bells. His welcome lasted for a week. He was immediately asked to serve at the Constitutional Convention, led by his friend George Washington, to draft the Constitution. The historical document listed the laws for governing the thirteen colonies which became the United States of America. There was also a Bill of Rights, which comprised the first ten amendments to the Constitution, guaranteeing the individual rights of the people. After the signing of the Constitution on September 17, 1787, Franklin lived for another three years. He spent most of the last year of his life ill in bed because he was so old and frail. He wrote Washington, "Though these years have been spent in excruciating pain, I am pleased that I have lived them, since they have brought me to see our present situation." By "present situation" he meant the new government that the Americans had formed that spring with Washington as president.

ᏆᎬᎢᎬᎨᏴᎾᎯᎬᎢᎬᎨᏴᎾᎯ Epilogue ᏅᎾᎯᎨᏴᎾᎯ

Death came to Benjamin Franklin on April, 17, 1790. He was eighty-four years old. One of his last public acts before he died was to sign a petition to the first Congress of the United States calling for an end to slavery. Twenty thousand people escorted Benjamin Franklin to his grave. He was buried next to his wife, Deborah. It was the kind of funeral that in the past had been reserved only for European royalty. The House of Representatives, which he founded, declared a one-month period of mourning. France, where he had been a beloved ambassador, went into public mourning. Thus died a friend of many people, including kings and queens, statesmen, politicians, writers, artists, and scientists. Franklin excelled among America's founding fathers. He was a writer, a diplomat, an inventor, a philosopher, a peacemaker—to name a few of his magnificent achievements. He was also the only American to have had a hand in drafting, negotiating, and signing all four of the documents establishing our nation's birth:

Declaration of Independence, July 4, 1776
Treaty of Alliance with France, February 6, 1778
Treaty of Peace with Great Britain, September 3, 1783
Constitution of the United States, September 17, 1787

THERE'S THE SCHOOL BELL!

THERE'S MY MOM!

DID YOU KNOW THAT FRANKLIN WAS TWENTY YEARS OLDER THAN THE OLDEST PERSON IN PHILADELPHIA WHEN HE DIED?

FRIENDSHIP SAYINGS of BENJAMIN FRANKLIN

1. The wise Man draws more Advantage from his Enemies, than the Fool from his Friends.

2. When a Friend deals with a Friend, Let the Bargain be clear and well penn'd, That they may continue Friends to the End.

3. Lend Money to an Enemy, and thou'lt gain him, to a Friend, and thou'lt lose him.

4. To be intimate with a foolish Friend, is like going to Bed to a Razor.

5. Friends are the true Scepters of Princes.

6. Friendship increases by visiting Friends, but by visiting seldom.

7. A false Friend and a Shadow, attend only while the Sun shines.

8. 'Tis great Confidence in a Friend to tell him your faults, greater to tell him his.

9. Some Worth, it argues, a Friend's Worth to know; Virtue to own the Virtue of a Foe.

10. He that sells upon trust, loses many friends, and always wants money.

11. Thou can'st not joke an Enemy into a Friend, but thou may'st a Friend into an Enemy.

12. Do good to thy Friend to keep him, to thy enemy to gain him.